MICHAEL PORTER'S VALUE CHAIN

Unlock your company's competitive advantage

Written by Xavier Robben
In collaboration with Amicie de Quatrebarbes
Translated by Carly Probert

Business 50MINUTES.com

50MINUTES.com

PROPEL
YOUR BUSINESS FORWARD!

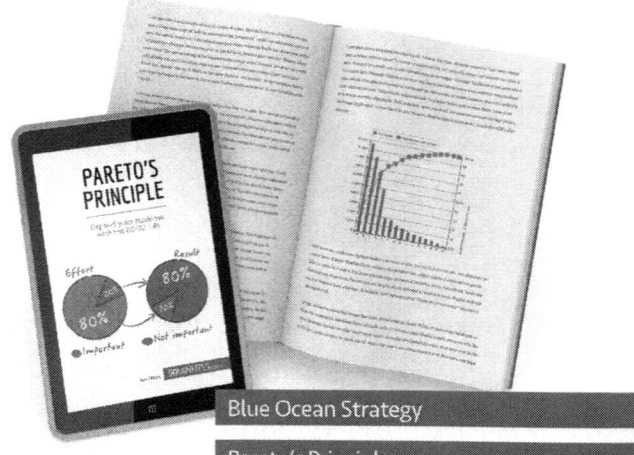

Blue Ocean Strategy

Pareto's Principle

Managing Stress at Work

Game Theory

www.50minutes.com

MICHAEL PORTER'S VALUE CHAIN — 1

Key information
Introduction

THEORY — 3

Value creation
Components
An adaptable model

LIMITATIONS AND EXTENSIONS — 10

Limitations and criticisms
Related models and extensions

PRACTICAL APPLICATION — 13

Advice and top tips
Case study – industrial company

SUMMARY — 24

FURTHER READING — 27

MICHAEL PORTER'S VALUE CHAIN

KEY INFORMATION

- **Names:** supply chain, value chain, supply chain management, Michael Porter's value chain.
- **Uses:** improving competitiveness, reducing costs, increasing value creation.
- **Why is it successful?** It is adaptable to all types of business, allows you to excel and provides clear, well-defined steps.
- **Key words:** competitive advantage, value creation, analytical tool, subdivision of activities.

INTRODUCTION

History

A professor of business strategy at Harvard, Michael E. Porter (born in 1947) considered the modern foundations of competitive strategy, competitiveness and the economic development of nations, states and religions.

In the 1980s, he began looking into the concept of competitive advantage and compiled his strategic theories, which were quickly adopted to improve corporate management, in the book *Competitive Advantage: Creating and Sustaining Superior Performance* (1985).

According to him, the superiority of a company comes from its mastery of competitive forces. These forces, more commonly known as 'Porter's five forces', are part of the essential factors of modern management. Later, Porter published *Competitive Strategy: Techniques for Analyzing Industries and Competitors* (1998), which mitigates his research on competitive strategy.

Definition of the model

The value chain is a series of actions, based on a sustainable economic approach, designed to establish and enhance a successful product or service in a market.

Any company, association or organisation that creates value that wants to improve its competitiveness can achieve its goals using the value chain. In fact, this model allows the entities concerned to successively analyse all of their activities in order to improve each step as much as possible to form and optimise a competitive advantage. This value chain is a valuable tool in strategic management as it works on the positioning of a product or service on the market.

Finally, the value chain aims to achieve three objectives:

- improvement of services
- cost reduction
- value creation.

THEORY

VALUE CREATION

Before starting to develop a competitive advantage, every company must learn the concept of value creation. This is an analytical system designed to break down the different functions of a company and examine the costs. The goal is to distribute resources throughout the chain as effectively as possible. This enables the strategic positioning of a product on the market based on its cost or differentiation.

How can you reduce costs? By adopting:

- an optimum manufacturing process
- the purchase of raw materials at a lower cost
- innovation
- the functionality of a product for greater differentiation
- better manufacturing quality
- improved customer service
- shorter delivery time thanks to good logistical organisation.

In addition to allowing a company to determine the process for achieving permanent profits, a good analysis of the different functions of the company can increase productivity and achieve sustainable and profitable growth.

COMPONENTS

There are nine major value-generating functions that make up Porter's model.

> **GOOD TO KNOW**
>
> The selection of value-generating activities is based on three criteria:
>
> - Do they rely on various economic mechanisms?
> - Do they constitute a considerable fraction of the costs?
> - Do they directly influence the competitive advantage?

They are divided into two categories:

- Firstly, there are five primary activities that directly affect the added value of the final product. This category includes the activities related to inbound logistics (1), operations (2), outbound logistics (3), marketing and sales (4) and services (5).
- Then there are four support activities which are indirectly involved in creating the final added value. These are the activities related to the company's infrastructure (1), human resources (2), technological development (3) and procurement (4).

Michael Porter's Value Chain

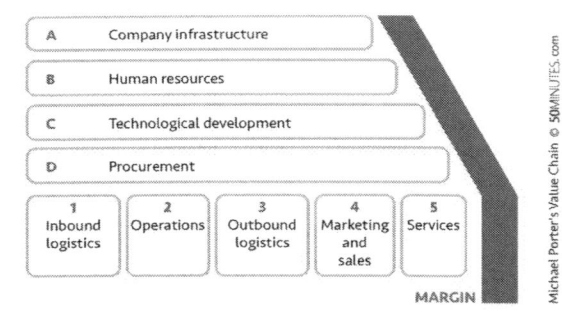

A	Company infrastructure
B	Human resources
C	Technological development
D	Procurement

1	2	3	4	5
Inbound logistics	Operations	Outbound logistics	Marketing and sales	Services

MARGIN

Porter represents the business using a simple graph, in which the primary activities are positioned vertically while the support activities are placed horizontally. The margin represents the difference between the final value of the product and all of the costs allocated to it (creation, launch, etc.). On the surface, the importance lies in the competitive advantage of each of the nine functions of the business. Of course, every company has its own graph which varies depending on many different factors – its nature, its industry, its position or even its efficiency.

> **GOOD TO KNOW**
>
> The competitive advantage of a company over its competitors can be seen through the comparison of value chains. The quality of an activity has a direct impact on costs, customer satisfaction and the importance of the

> margin. The analysis of a function does not always give a positive result. In fact, some of them can reduce the value or be worth less than competitors.

Primary activities (basic activities)

The primary activities are the main functions organised within a company. They contribute directly to the creation of the product, marketing actions, sales policy, delivery to the end customer and the after-sales service. Although each business does not operate in the same way, most of them have these five primary activities:

- **(1) Inbound logistics** brings together the procedure for acquiring resources, including raw materials, their receipt, stock entry, etc.
- **(2) Operations** involve the use of raw materials, production of goods, quality testing, packaging, maintenance, etc.
- **(3) Outbound logistics** includes the output of inventory, order preparation, delivery to distributors and end customers, etc.
- **(4) Marketing and sales** includes promotion, communication, pricing, advertising, distribution channel management, etc.
- **(5) Services** involve repair, maintenance, after-sales services, etc.

> **GOOD TO KNOW**
>
> These activities, however, are not independent of one another. Good control of one component can have positive implications for other elements of the chain. The various functions are interconnected and can cause a series of consequences when there are changes to activities. These connections, which often go unnoticed, play an important role in cost management and competitive advantage.

Support activities

Support activities contribute to the smooth running of operations by giving the company the opportunity to perform the primary activities and manage the coordination, in order to maximise efficiency. Among them are:

- **(A) Company infrastructure**, which includes general, financial and administrative management, the legal department and the department in charge of planning, quality control, etc.
- **(B) Human resources**, which is involved in recruitment, training, remuneration processes, skills management, organisation structure, bonus policy, layoffs, etc.
- **(C) Research and development** includes research and technology selection, ability to innovate, development of products or services, product safety, patent management, etc.
- **(D) Procurement (or supply)** involves methods of purchasing raw materials, sourcing suppliers, negotiations

with suppliers, rental of premises, etc.

Support activities may affect certain primary activities. However, the functions described are not present in every company, even if they are common.

> **GOOD TO KNOW**
>
> It is theoretically preferable for companies to use Porter's value chain before choosing their strategy and positioning for each product. However, it is common for the situation to be chronologically reversed.

AN ADAPTABLE MODEL

When defining this concept, Porter stresses the urgent need for a personal schematisation. He advises companies to first choose between a short or long value chain, depending on certain activities' importance or lack thereof. Sometimes it is also necessary to reorganise the value chain in order to differentiate yourself from competitors. Finally, Porter points out that the key to competitive advantage lies as much in the reorganising of activities as the interconnections. Indeed, if one of the activities is progressing independently of the others, there may be an imbalance between the different components that generates new costs.

GOOD TO KNOW

Although the terminology used to present the concept is primarily focused on the vocabulary relating to product manufacturing – 'storage', 'production' or 'repair' – the value chain works just as well with companies that provide services.

LIMITATIONS AND EXTENSIONS

LIMITATIONS AND CRITICISMS

Although several decades old, Porter's model remains very relevant: it still provides today the necessary tools for companies looking for an increase in the added value of their activities as well as a reduction in their production costs. Nonetheless, despite its effectiveness, the value chain is increasingly subject to criticism because it does have certain limits.

Firstly, the implementation of this method is relatively long and complicated:

- the amount of data required to use the value chain is immense and often difficult to obtain;
- the margin of interpretation is too large, which may damage analysis and distort the final result;
- the lack of precision could affect the analysis.

Secondly, the desire to hold competitive advantage in a market drives businesses to adopt cost management policies, which in itself is one of the main limitations of the model. In fact, if all companies use this cost management strategy, the proposed price will get lower and lower, but companies cannot reduce costs indefinitely.

Thirdly, it is difficult to determine the concept of value creation linked to this chain because the value itself is perceived differently by different economists:

- Neoclassical economics (early 19th century) is based on the subjective utility or the relative value linked to the exchange and non-exchange of production costs. In other words, the value of a product depends on the value of another product in the same market.
- This is opposed by classical economics (between 1760 and 1848, in France and England), which perceives the value as absolute and determined according to the characteristics of the object.

Ostensibly closer to neoclassical thinking, Porter's model is based on the interpretation of the customer's will. More broadly, critics of Michael E. Porter accuse him of an overall lack of clarity and precision in his definitions. They also condemn the lack of empirical data needed, according to them, to justify his theories.

These limits and criticisms of Porter's model are not exhaustive and, furthermore, many agree that the foundations of the chain have been complemented by the work of other less renowned economists. Finally, even if it is used with care, Porter's value chain remains very much a tool of utmost importance in corporate management.

RELATED MODELS AND EXTENSIONS

Porter's five forces

Michael Porter has always tried to understand the issues related to competition. Thus, a few years before the publication of his research on the value chain, he realised that the competitive structure of a company is too narrowly defined.

He also established, in 1979, a model called 'Porter's five forces'. This concept allows you to maintain competitive advantage and ensure some long-term profitability. These forces are:

- **Competition intensity between companies in the sector.** Companies within the same sector fight to keep their position.
- **Suppliers' bargaining power.** The more powerful a supplier, the more he can impose conditions (price, quality, quantity) and vice versa for the suppliers who have little influence.
- **Customers' bargaining power.** They impose requirements on price, service and quality. Therefore, they influence the profitability of a market.
- **Threat of new market entrants.** It depends on the size of the market (economy of scale), the desire for business diversification, the cost of entry, access to raw materials, technical standards, etc. New competitors inevitably upset the hierarchy of market players.
- **Threat of substitution products.** They represent an alternative to the market supply and are generally better value for money.

Note that each of the components of this model is directly influenced by the law and regulations set by public authorities.

PRACTICAL APPLICATION

ADVICE AND TOP TIPS

Unlike general accounting, the value chain is not legally binding, but it remains an important tool in corporate management. While there are different methods that do not contravene the law, it is highly advisable to use the traditional method, detailed below, in six steps.

Setting up the analysis

The first phase is to determine the field to be examined. This requires a good understanding of the manufacturing process according to the value chain and identifying all the connections between the different activities. Then you must define the starting point (the raw material suppliers) and the end point (the stock of finished products or the customer) of the overall processes of the company.

Mapping out the current value chain

Secondly, you must draw the representative value chain of the company, starting from point A to point Z, remembering to include all the different stages. Generally, these stages are illustrated by squares, stocks by triangles and transfers shown by arrows.

Illustration of a value chain

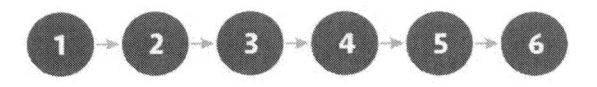

1 → 2 → 3 → 4 → 5 → 6

This value chain, greatly simplified, can represent central purchasing (1), which sends the goods stocked for purchase (2). The goods are then sent to the workshop (3) where they undergo quality control (4), before joining the stock of finished products (5). Once the products are ordered, they go to the distribution area (6).

Collecting authentic data

This step aims to gather relevant information on all the activities and connections, but also to verify their authenticity. The data to be collected differs from one company to another according to its structure and sector. For example, a service company is not concerned about manufacturing processes, unlike an industrial company. Industries must learn more about the length of an activity cycle, the number of workers needed for each phase, the transfer distance and duration between each step, the cost of activities, the efficiency of machinery used, inventory turnover, the value of assets, the ratio of defective products, etc.

Submitting the diagram and data

It is then useful to discuss the planned value chain with the people concerned. You should, for example, ask workers their views on the diagram of manufacturing. In fact, the team members may have a different view of the process of the company, and consulting them may rectify misinterpreted aspects. It is recommended at this stage to add the duration of execution and the duration of evaluation to the diagram. The first estimates the time required to complete the course of the process while the second measures the time for incorporating value. The comparison between these two data can help identify areas for improvement.

Restructuring the value chain

For the fifth step, you must look at the list of questions established in 1999 by Mike Rother and John Shook: answering them allows the company to review and possibly redesign the value chain. The eight themes addressed by these two economists are intended to promote competitive advantage. The purpose of this phase is essentially to change or eliminate activities that create little or no value. The closer the execution period is to the development period, the more the company has succeeded in reducing its unnecessary transfers. Once the optimum (or balance) is established, it's time to represent the company through a restructured value chain.

Mike Rother and John Shook's eight questions are:

- What is the duration of the value chain?
- Is the production kept in a store or is it sent directly to the shipping bay?
- In which parts of the value chain can we establish a continuous flow?

- Where can it resort to flow systems (pull approach) with a store?
- What specific point of the production chain will be chosen as a 'regulatory process' for scheduling production?
- How will you refine production?
- What area of the work will be used a regulatory process time unit?
- What related process improvements will be required?

> **GOOD TO KNOW: PUSH AND PULL**
>
> Push and pull flows are the flow of goods, merchandise or other components stemming from forecasts. The first are driven by forecasts while the latter are generated by customer orders.

Once you have answered these questions, it is important to:

- diagnose the competitive advantage based on a competitive value chain on the market;
- assimilate the different assets of the company;
- assess the value-creating activities;
- consider that competitive advantage comes not only from the performance of each activity, but also the interconnections between them.

Planning improvement actions

Once the company has determined the activities for potential improvement, it must find the means to allow it to improve its performance. It is advised to base this on the redesigned diagram and list all the tasks of the nine activities (primary and support). From suppliers to the first modifications, the company will have to reset the follow-up analysis at each stage from the starting point. Indeed, a redesigned activity can have an impact on the others because of their interconnections. These modifications are capable of impacting a company's value chain.

The success of this analysis loop, where the starting point is always the same, is based on four rules:

- the designed process is continuous and respects the production cycle;
- the chain allows for the control of simple and efficient production;
- the company benefits from improvements regarding expense and order management;
- the execution speed increases while the volume of stored stock is reduced.

Advice

Porter's value chain is a common tool in the field of management; however it does not always work when it is subject to confusion. The most common errors are:

- being imprecise when identifying the scope of the value chain;
- developing a value chain from a diagram that distorts the graph at the level of the relationships between activities;
- forgetting a step in the value chain. It is therefore highly advisable to physically trace the product's journey within

the company, from the stocks of raw materials to the shipping of the finished product, to ensure that each step is fully included in the analysis.

CASE STUDY – INDUSTRIAL COMPANY

Value chain of the case study company

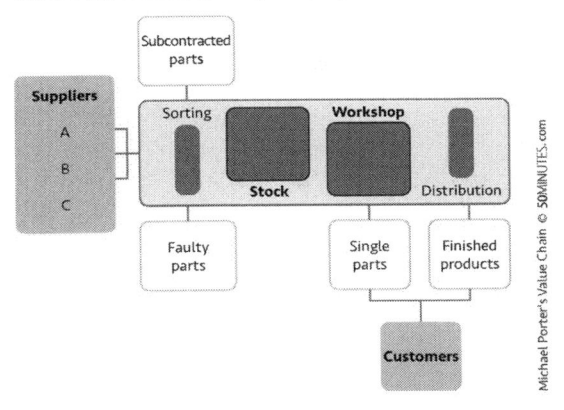

Michael Porter's Value Chain © 50MINUTES.com

Context

Although Porter's model is not restricted to industrial companies, we chose to use the example of a steel company that involves a long value chain. This steel company fought hard to acquire its place as a worldwide market leader. In addition to mergers and other acquisitions, it is able to adapt to the market that enabled it to establish itself within this niche market. The company used various methods to refine its business management, including the value chain.

Its main activity is the assembly of various machines/tools that can carve fine threads on steel tubes. Once assembled together, they allow customers to extract gas or oil.

The company buys its raw materials (steel and cast iron) and outsourced parts from various suppliers. Purchases are stored before being redirected to the sorting centre where they must pass a compliance test. Once verified, they are stored in a space called 'company-owned stock'. The parts are then sent to the workshop. For this company, managing stocks is a complicated task since only 80% of the parts are identical from one machine to the other. Customers have their own tubes to which the device must be able to adapt. Manufacturing the product is a very complex process and takes between four and six months. Once completed, the machines are stored before undergoing a series of tests to ensure that they work properly. They are then packed to avoid as much damage as possible, and transported to their final destination. Moreover, the company is also involved in the repair of poorly calibrated, defective or outdated equipment.

This manufacturing process, developed more than 25 years ago, is still used today, although it is not exactly the same. Indeed, the company has reorganised its structure to improve its results, despite the complexity and high cost of doing so. This was a necessary decision for the company to retain its position as a world leader in the sector.

Reorganisation of the value chain within the company

To undertake a full review of its organisation situation, the company used an external team consisting of qualified experts in management:

- In association with the managers, they started out by mapping out the activities to analyse and selecting a starting point (the receipt of raw materials) and an end point (delivery to customers). It was necessary, however, to connect the fifth core business activity with the third; since after repairing machines in the fifth activity, they are redirected to the customer.
- They then designed the value chain, taking care to indicate the steps (squares), stock (triangles) and transport (arrows).
- The external team then prepared a 20-page questionnaire on the criteria of the company to gather accurate data based on areas of business activity. Managers, along with their engineers, first answered the questions specific to their area. Then, to check and adjust the data, experts made this information available to all workers. Their comments clarified the previously provided answers. The external team also estimated the length of time of execution and recovery in order to identify potential causes for delay: after comparison, the findings pointed to the fact that the execution time was too long.

Answers to the questions from Mike Rother and John Shook allowed the experts to target the various shortcomings of the steel company's value chain. So, the company has discovered the following facts:

- Its competitive advantage on the value chain comes from the efficient management of raw materials stocks.
- Its assets were essentially based on production costs linked to the excellent workforce and productivity of machines.
- There were two points for potential improvement, one on the manufacturing level, the other on the organisational level. The first revealed a large number of machines were not appropriate for customer demands while the second showed the time between phases and stock areas was too long.
- Many pieces broke during the manufacturing process. This is not due to a production malfunction, but to the purchases made in advance of the chain, and, more precisely, the outsourced items.

After the schematic improvement from Porter's value chain provided by the experts, the company noted three major changes:

- reduction of machine manufacturing time
- reduction of manufacturing costs
- improvement in the supply of finished products, which are more consistent with customer expectations.

By theoretically and physically analysing the different production routes, the company was then able to improve some activities to optimise results and maintain its leading position on the market.

Reasons for global leadership

- **Coordination with customers.** A major problem encountered by the company was the lack of precision in the execution of customer orders. In fact, the machines had to carve threads on the tubes available in the workshop, even if the diameter of the tube did not always correspond to customer requirements. They then had to return to the company for adjustments. This obvious organisational problem was solved by constructing a warehouse reserved for the customers' tubes. The machines can now operate accurately and the company is no longer worried about complaints.
- **The company's organisation.** In the beginning, the company was just a small business with a few employees. Over the years it has seen its number of orders increase exponentially. The company has grown gradually by increasing the areas of stock and the number of spaces dedicated to workshops and offices. Thus, when the first local branch became too small to carry out operations, the company built a second, then a third, where the raw materials and finished products were carefully stored. The experts noted that the journeys of heavy stock were too long between the first premises (used for manufacturing) and the third, and how the initial stocks had to cross the entire workshop to reach the location for assembly line operation. The company then decided to reverse the functions of the first two warehouses. By arranging them according to the workflow, this has reduced the distances between the workshop, inventory areas and sorting and control centres.

- **The improvement of the outsourced parts**. The statistics reported a number of broken pieces that was too high. The analyses showed that these came mostly from subcontractors in Eastern Europe. The problem was the quality of their raw materials. For the company to remain competitive, it was not possible to manufacture these mechanical parts themselves or change its providers, since all of them were relatively more expensive. To ensure quality, the company now buys raw materials from suppliers in France that it sends to the Czech Republic and Poland to manufacture its parts. Although the company has seen the cost of purchases rise, it benefits from a reduction of the number of orders.

Without these significant changes, the company could not have remained a worldwide market leader. The redesign of the value chain involved complex decisions which, although expensive, have proven beneficial to the entire company.

SUMMARY

- The concept of the value chain developed by Professor Michael E. Porter appeared in 1985 in his book *Competitive Advantage: Creating and Sustaining Superior Performance*.
- The value chain is a business management model that locates the creation of value within a company.
- This analytical tool allows all companies to analyse all their activities in succession to identify and improve the less efficient areas in order to maximise competitive advantage.
- The value chain divides the company into nine activities, belonging to two categories: five primary activities and four support activities.
- The value chain analysis takes place in six stages: identifying the area to examine, drawing the value chain, collection and authentication of information, reorganisation of the chain and action planning.
- This tool has many advantages: it is adaptable to all types of companies; it improves competitiveness; it provides clear and well defined steps to effectively carry out the chain analysis, etc.
- However, evaluation is a long process, requiring a large amount of data. Furthermore, personal interpretation plays an important role, which may make the model less accurate.
- The value chain is consistent with other equally important models in business management, including the famous 'Porter's five forces'.
- The value chain is a powerful tool, but should be used

with caution. For it to be effective, it is important to understand that each analysis differs from one company to the next.
- Improving the value chain involves complex decisions which, when done well, allow companies to achieve their goals.

We want to hear from you!
Leave a comment on your online library
and share your favourite books on social media!

FURTHER READING

BIBLIOGRAPHY

- Hartwich, F., Devlin, J. and Kormawa, P. (2011) *Industrial value chain diagnostics: an integrated tool*. Under the direction of the United Nations Industrial Development Organization: Vienna.
- Lachat, D. (2007) La Chaîne de valeur, modèles entrepreneuriaux et étalonnage. *Halshs Archives ouvertes*. [Online]. [Accessed 23 May 2014]. Available from: <http://halshs.archives-ouvertes.fr/docs/00/12/44/39/PDF/Chaines_de_valeur_modeles_entrepreneuriaux_et_etalon_.pdf>
- Magreta, J. (2012) *La Méthode Michael Porter*. Montreal: Éditions Transcontinental.
- Porter, M. E. (1998) *Competitive Advantage: Creating and Sustaining Superior Performance*. New York: Simon & Schuster.
- Porter, M. E. (2010) The Five Competitive Forces That Shape Strategy. *Harvard Business Review*.
- Rother, M. and Shook, J. (1999) *Learning to see: Value Stream Mapping to Add Value and Eliminate MUDA*. Cambridge: The Lean Entreprise Institute of Brookline Massachusetts.
- Zeroual, T. (2011) Supply Chain Management : portée et limites. L'Apport des théories des réseaux. *ESCE de Paris*.

ADDITIONAL SOURCES

- Harvard Business Review. (2011) *HBR's 10 Must Reads on Strategy*. Boston: Harvard Business School Publishing.
- Magretta, J. (2012) *Understanding Michael Porter: The Essential Guide to Competition and Strategy*. Boston: Harvard Business School Publishing.

50MINUTES.com

- History
- Business
- Coaching

IMPROVE YOUR GENERAL KNOWLEDGE
IN A BLINK OF AN EYE !

www.50minutes.com

© 50MINUTES.com, 2016. All rights reserved.

www.50minutes.com

Ebook EAN: 9782806265906

Paperback EAN: 9782806270061

Legal Deposit: D/2015/12603/430

Cover: © Primento

Digital conception by Primento, the digital partner of publishers.

Printed in Poland
by Amazon Fulfillment
Poland Sp. z o.o., Wrocław